The Prints of
JAMES ENSOR

The Prints of
JAMES ENSOR

From the Collection of H. Shickman
(Formerly Franck Collection, Antwerp)

Introduction by Professor Louis Lebeer

DA CAPO PRESS • NEW YORK • 1971

In Cooperation with H. Shickman Gallery, New York

PUBLISHER'S NOTE

The collection represented in this catalog was originally assembled by François Franck, a close friend of Ensor's and one of his earliest patrons. It later passed to Charles Franck and was shown for the first time in 1960 at the Museum am Ostwall in Dortmund, Germany, on the occasion of the centenary of the artist's birth. Shortly thereafter it was acquired by Mr. H. Shickman. It is probably the most complete collection of Ensor's graphic oeuvre in the United States. It is missing only Ensor's one lithograph, one soft-ground etching, and a handful of less important prints, mostly late ones. (The missing prints are illustrated in the Supplement to this catalog.) The publishers are grateful to Professor Louis Lebeer for permitting us to include as an introduction to this catalog a translation of his monograph, *James Ensor, Aquafortiste,* published originally by the Ministère de l'Instruction Publique, Antwerp, in 1952.

INTRODUCTION

James Ensor's work is a blessing for writers as well as for art critics, for all who are intrigued by the mysteries of the mind and touched by the delights of beauty. Ensor's personality as revealed in his work can be subjected to an inexhaustible variety of interpretations. His vivid imagination is so subtly shifting that those who attempt to catch it precisely are always surprised. What can be evoked instantly by a picture can only be described in words by listing separate details, thus fragmenting visions and concealing, in a false verbal coherence, the eddies of a soul and heart so complex as to appear contradictory.

James Ensor was at once so tragic and so humorous, so serious and so mischievous, so sincere and so malicious, so harsh and so benevolent, so provoking and so tormented, so mocking and so tender, so amorous and so independent, so realistic and so visionary, that it is possible to understand him only through a deep and direct study of his work. Here we discover his greatness, his strength, his originality—and sometimes, his weaknesses. The character of his personality and his spirit underlie that of his art, in which we sense his understanding of the revelations of Bosch, Brueghel, Rembrandt, Goya, Turner, Constable, Hogarth, Gilbray, Rowlandson, Whistler, and Van Gogh—a list anyone may expand almost as he likes, for James Ensor worked in the tradition and line of all the great masters. Yet he attained the universal in lonely wonder at the elements which made up his life: the sea, nature, light; his house filled with shells, chinoiseries, masks; and his city, enlivened by the extravagances of the Carnaval, by processions and parades. Observing it, he recreated it after his own vision, by his own hand—the vital, palpable beauty of material, of color, of form, of light. He was assailed by strange, dream-like images which awakened in him unfathomable mental experiences. As all great masters, he was both part of an ongoing tradition and the precursor of a new one.

In truth the subject is too deep—the more we delve into it, the richer it becomes. But we must be careful not to press the artist beyond the ideas with which he was concerned and of which he was aware; to see that the object of our continuing admiration lies in the art which he practiced with such fine sensibility. How otherwise can we understand that his art is great not only because of his powerful creative imagination, but also because of the clear and captivating authority with which he practiced the various means of expression which he chose in order to give form to his visions of nature and to the dictates of his spirit? Through these gifts, he became both one of the great colorists among painters of our era and one of the greatest artists in etching and drypoint.

One might have thought that Ensor's vision would have required subtle color modulations, that "Ensorian light" could not exist beyond the quivering play of his colors, had not his etchings and his drypoints shown that a few strokes, even a few dots, were sufficient for him to reveal the very essence of that light and of its effect on bodies and objects. Only a few strokes were enough for him to communicate to us his visions and dreams—to show the action of light on subjects observed with eyes able to spiritualize matter, able to strip these subjects of everything except what renders them alive in light.

In Ensor's paintings, everything indicates that he was himself carried away by the magic of his colors. In his engravings, on the other hand, he saw nothing with the eye of the paintaer, saw only line and the values of black and white which belong to the realm of the mind's eye.

Engraving, like drawing, is the art of expressing through line and form a clear-sighted awareness which has been awakened by some natural phenomenon or suggested by the imagination. "You must be willing to see in order to see," wrote Paul Valêry, "and this willingness has drawing both as its end and its means." Similarly, Max Jacob suggested that "we understand by drawing the desire to express a form. The stronger and more reasoned the desire, the more beautiful the drawing." And Charles Baudelaire properly maintained that "we must not forget that etching is a profound, dangerous, treacherous art, which reveals the faults of an artist's character as clearly as it does his virtues."

The line, drawn or engraved—that almost disembodied line—always represents only the sheer desire toward expression, sheer will. It would be of nothing more than symbolic interest or interest as psychological documentation, and certainly not of artistic interest, were it not enlivened by sensibility. "Engraving does not struggle to emulate life," wrote Henri Foçillon, "but transposes it into a register of two notes whose chords are more imperious than all the vast resources of the whole range of colors." This is to say nothing more than that drawing or that engraving is the formidable process by which the artist surrenders himself unconditionally, revealing exactly what he *sees,* what he is completely *willing to express,* what his hand is able to evoke by a line. Diderot was wrong when he called Rembrandt's etchings "quick scribbles," even if, in saying this, he was not contradicting Alain, who believed that "the lines of a drawing are not in any way an imitation of the lines of an object—rather, they are the residue of gestures which grasp and express the form of the object. That is why one can recognize in a drawing the artist as well as the model." The act, the gesture, the line, the stroke are so important that it is taken for granted that we must judge them, admire them, appreciate them in themselves for the enchantment of their own special beauty, for their power to evoke and reveal.

Altogether, James Ensor made 133 prints with his own hand—117 etchings, fourteen drypoints, one soft-ground etching, and one lithograph. It was in 1886 that he took an etching needle in his hand for the first time. Immediately he produced eight plates. In 1887 he published eleven, and in 1888—the year in which he painted his *Christ's Entry Into Brussels*—he made no less than forty-five. Thereafter, his work in the area of prints gradually slackened. From 1889 through 1904, he signed hardly more than two or three editions a year, and ended by abandoning prints entirely until 1933-34, when, more at the urgent request of a collector avid for rarities than impelled by the need to create, he "scribbled" on the copper—this was now really the case—three drypoints, *Lady Godiva, The Old House,* and *The Procession at Ghistelles,* slight works however you may wish to look at them. And though in 1934 he made one more print, *The Devil at the Mill,* a soft-ground etching made on a plate which Roger Hebbelynck guaranteed would bite, this was only to promote the success of a collection of *Tales* by Horace Van Offel published by George Hoyoux. A sin of old age!

As this summary suggests, Ensor created his major etchings and drypoints during the years in which he had revealed himself as a master capable of bringing reality to the world of the unreal, of placing immediate observation in the service of an unbridled imagination; during the years in which his troubled mind located the most tormented aberrations, even among phenomena which appeared at first to belong only to an interior atmosphere of calm and intimacy. After 1900, Ensor could no longer carry on the struggle. Thereafter he remained stationary, his work often uneven artistically, although he was still the great spinner of fantasies, still mischievous and even malicious, ever the great landscapist, the great creator of seascapes, as he had already been very early in his career.

In the entire oeuvre of James Ensor, the etchings and drypoints occupy a very special place, not only because of their original beauty, but also because they often complete and detail the characteristics of the vision, if not the facture, of a great many of his paintings. However, if Ensor was inspired to rework one canvas or another as a print some years after initial execution of the canvas, he was also inspired—in one instance after an interval of several years—to translate one etching or another into a painting—a painting faithful to the vision underlying the print. This presents a considerable problem for those who attempt to establish, not so much a chronology, but a logical and continuous evolutionary sequence for Ensor's style and work—his somber period, his clear period, etc. For instance, the vocative drypoint, *Christ Calming the Storm,* made in 1886, served as a prototype for paintings made in 1890 and 1891; *Boats at Low Tide,* engraved in 1888, did not tempt the artist's brushes until 1900; and *The Gamblers,* laid on copper in 1895, was not transferred to canvas until 1902. On the other hand, *The Entry of Christ Into Brussels,* painted in 1888, became an etching in 1898, while *Beggars Warming Themselves,* a painting from 1882, was not reworked as an etching until 1895, along with other works of the same spirit. *Angry Masks,* painted in 1883, took its place as an engraving only in 1895.

Except for a small number of etchings, in which the "bleeding" caused by the work of the acid has resulted in the sacrifice of graphic clarity to the vagaries of more complex tonal values, Ensor's prints are generally marked by a linear purity. Anything limiting the degree of clarity, or the fineness of line, detracts directly from the atmosphere, or, one might say, the tonality in which the artist conceives and contemplates—spiritually or in actuality—the idea or the event which inspires him.

No graphic work by Ensor has a light as clear and moving as his first plate, *The Mocking of Christ* (1886). Whenever Ensor presents an episode in the life of Christ, he always makes that marvelous apparition shine with a light that is radiant, supernatural, magical. The very manner in which he uses light, breaking up with rare animation the contours of forms in space, is incisive evidence of the conscious and sensitive mastery with which he employed the etcher's needle from the very beginning. And do we not, in praising this first print, recall the name of Rembrandt, so that we may better recommend that of Ensor? Yet he lacked in this work—at the very beginning, if you will—a steady technique, the ability to place and to move with absolute certainty the line itself—the very line which moves in all of its evocative force in that immensely powerful seascape, *Christ Calming the Storm* (1886).

The latter must be judged as it was when simply a drypoint, before it was etched, if we are to feel and admire its subtle richness, its sensitive power, its impressionistic luminosity. Then we discover everything that a line placed by drypoint can convey in delicate modulations of accent, in suggestive transparencies, all brought to life by the pure surface of a paper which, reacting to the arrangement of the strokes, to the interlacing and bending of the lines, is able to evoke at one and the same time water and air, atmosphere and light.

If the bite of the acid detracted here from the deliberate subtlety and sustained delicacy of the original work, this certainly was not the case in other instances when James Ensor expressed himself through etching. The *Large View of Mariakerke* (1887) and, even better, *The Fishing Docks at Ostend* (1888) show this clearly. No work has ever been able to evoke better than the latter, with such an economy of material means and so conscious a style, light in all of its quivering vibrations, in its pulverizing action—and to do so without destroying lines and contours. It is a work of the purest impressionism—not of an analytical impressionism, where the structure of the forms is lost, but of an impressionism where the life of light is revealed in its special and particular activity, outside of momentary or accidental atmospheric conditions, and without the colors which, by its capricious reflections, it causes constantly to change.

Engraving could not be otherwise—pure and original engraving, that is. Original engraving, in fact, has implicit the vision to grasp the permanent, the exactly repeatable, in a natural event, since it involves viewing the event in large measure with the mind's eye, with a vision which, in order to retain only the constant, formal elements of a subject, abstracts underlying reality from accidental aspects or conditions, from transient details which physical eyes are able to accept. James Ensor firmly adheres to this outlook in presenting *The Fishing Docks at Ostend,* where the quivering action of the light is rendered by a vibrant swarm of minute lines and dots, following the outline of lines and contours from the point at which the living forms are born. It is not magical that a few strokes and dots should cause the paper to intensify the light and to show us the sky above, an arm of the sea below?

In spite of the distortions of the etching process, and in spite of the fact that Ensor's vision darkened and became more heavily luminous, the theme of his inspiration carried him forward. *The Ice Skaters* (1889), set on the property of Ernest Rousseau, is based upon the same expressive resource, although in the same year, Ensor made, in a much lighter, clearer fashion, *The Windmill at Mariakerke,* another example of the power with which strokes sensitively selected and applied are able to evoke the presence of different materials—sand and dry vegetation, for instance—revealed, nevertheless, in a dazzling light.

It is, moreover, in his landscapes, engraved after such a diversity of views, that Ensor presents his greatest subtlety. *The Large View of Mariakerke* (1887), *Boats at Low Tide* (1888; and executed as a painting only in 1900), *The Orchard* (1886), *The Channel of Nieuport* (1888), *The Beach at La Panne* (1904), portray experiences with nature in which, with a facture sometimes heavy in emphasis, sometimes subtly sensitive in line, sometimes extreme in economy, Ensor could capture forms, suggest volumes, establish planes; could recall hours gone by, the seasons, the weather; could evoke substances, enliven the atmosphere—in short, elicit the poetry in the events he witnessed.

To be able to appreciate, and therefore to admire, the printed oeuvre of James Ensor as it deserves, it is not possible to be satisfied only with knowing the subjects which inspired him; it is necessary all the more to pierce the mystery and discover the miraculous things he could achieve with a stroke; it is necessary to sharpen our own perception in order to "see" his impulses and his will to expression. If Ensor knew how to guide a line with the utmost lightness and delicacy, he also knew how to make a line heavy whenever the tonality of the work called for it to be heavy. See, for instance, *Beggars Warming Themselves* (1895), as well as *Skeletons Warming Themselves* (1895) and *The Gamblers,* all etchings which refer to paintings created between 1882 and 1885, at the time of his most somber outlook, but which themselves date from 1895. It is not better to distrust dates when trying to establish and explain the evolution of Ensor's art? And how admirable is the manner in which Ensor's hand knew how to guide, accumulate, interlace, interrupt, enliven, and sweep into arabesques clean lines, in order to evoke the life and spirit of bodies and objects, to create space, to enliven forms, to establish the brightness and the clear or heavy nature of light, to evoke color in a situation in which it is absent because it is unnecessary!

Ensor did not really need other means to give shape to his most diverse inspirations, even those which were suggested to him by reality. Portraiture, for example; with an exceptionally keen eye, Ensor simultaneously observed and remembered the personal conformation, the material values, the luminous movements, and the psychological traits of a model. This is evident in his portrait of the Scandinavian botanist *Frise* (1886) and that of his great friend *Ernest Rousseau* (1887). The latter is a masterpiece of vision, of sensibility, of bold technique. Ensor, who always understood how to select his medium, executed this portrait in drypoint.

Rarely has this medium been able to breathe so much truth into a face and rarely has a face been illuminated with such transparency, as well as with a black as perilously rich.

James Ensor was several times his own portraitist; but his self-portraits were not always drawn directly from nature. On one occasion (1889) he worked from a photograph and ended up by replacing his own head with a skull. It is impossible to ignore the place occupied by death in Ensor's tormented imagination. In 1888, he made a self-portrait of himself as a skeleton, which, according to him, was just how he would look in 1960; a little etching, made with only a few strokes, but so unmercifully realistic that it ran the risk of having its wit overlooked—a small masterpiece of pure design. He also portrayed himself in the gleam of a lamp in a room (1886). This fascinating example of impressionistic intimacy was a prediction, as it were, which prepares us to see the domestic calm of this corner of his room transformed into the horror which could provoke his *Haunted Closet* (1888), a print haunted by death. The specter of death never let go of Ensor. He saw it everywhere; he submitted to the inescapable empire which leads man to his fatal end; he portrayed it, armed with a great scythe, *Pursuing Humanity* (1896).

The master of masks and skeletons was constantly compelled to show the human crowd. In his works based on episodes from the Gospels he consciously chose themes in which Christ appears with crowds—*Feeding of the Five Thousand* (1891), for instance. Another time, he invites us to be present at the *Entry of Christ Into Brussels* (1898), while on yet another occasion an immense crowd swarms around a *Cathedral* (1886). By a marvel of drawing, he always succeeds in these crowd scenes in individualizing each one of the figures, although the entire group seems only a compact and unified mass, just as through a technical tour de force, he prevents the varnish from peeling during the engraving process and does not blur the tangle of very meaningful little lines.

To discover the outrageous, mischievous, malicious, mocking Ensor, we must turn every time to those grotesque, hallucinated dreams to which he gave a form and which people like to consider as pre-Surrealist. If such works as *Bizarre Musicians* (1888) did not suggest serious intentions, one would be tempted to consider them as caricatures, since very often they are inspired by people encountered by Ensor in real life, to whom he often lent faces recalling the masks from the shop which, from his earliest years, had surrounded him and had never left him. If he had the opportunity, he hardly ever restrained himself from presenting derogatory images of particular professions which were normally held in high esteem—hence, *The Policemen* (1888), *The Good Judges* (1894), *The Wicked Physicians* (1895), and their colleagues, "Iston, Poulfamatus," etc., whom he mocks by showing them occupied in examining the excrement of Darius (1886). Ensor was quite aware that the human face takes on different masks when he dreamed of the vices of which man can be the pitiful victim. And it is in compositions of this sort that his stroke and line assume a style which is the most expressive, the most tortuous, the most extraordinary.

The Master of Ostend is fantastic, in the most comprehensive sense, when he gives form to his obsession with diabolical forces. He admits that he is portraying himself in *Demons Taunting Me* (1895); furthermore, he invites us to follow the demons on their *Infernal Procession* (1887), a work of rare linear purity which, not surprisingly, brings to mind the name of Hieronymous Bosch. Again, he sees them lead *Christ In Hell* (1895) and goads them to take vengeance on Him in *Christ Tormented by Demons* (1895). Of course, the question has always been raised as to the extent these diabolical themes were suggested to the artist by the literature of the time. That might have been true, yet the creator of so many other fantasies—one must remember *Tormenting the Elephant* (1888), *Wizards in the Whirlwind* (1888), and the like—had worked here too under the domination of tormented visions, visions so personal that they can only be properly called Ensorian. The fact is, however, that more than one of Ensor's works was directly inspired by literature. Two titles alone—*King Pest* (1895) and *Hop Frog's Revenge* (1898) testify that the great artist was an attentive reader of Edgar Allen Poe.

One of James Ensor's friends asked him one day why he made etchings. He replied that "the fragility of paintings frightens me, vulnerable as they are to the mishaps of the restorer, to general hazards, to the distortions of reproductions—I want to live, to speak for a long time yet to the men of tomorrow. I think of solid copper plates, of inks which cannot be altered, of simple reproductions, of faithful impressions, and therefore I have taken etching as my means of expression."

Could we not say, therefore, that from the moment that James Ensor discovered engraving, he decided that for his own future glory and for the pleasure "of the men of tomorrow," it was useless to continue painting? If this actually was the motive for Ensor's taking up engraving, he was simply letting himself in for bitter disillusionment. He might have realized this had he been there when the last impressions of his etchings were taken, had he seen the actual conditions of his "solid copper plates." Certainly he knew that the surface of metal is as vulnerable, as "fragile" as the color coating of a canvas or panel; of course he knew that the engraved surface of a copper plate is also exposed to the mistakes of the man who retouches it, to the inadequacy and calumnies of the printer, to the distortions of late impressions. Why otherwise did he color them so often? And the paper, that humble little sheet of paper, without which the most beautiful copper plate can never produce a beautiful print, is much more "alterable," indeed, destructible, than the most questionable canvas, which can always be replaced by a better one if the coat of paint above is endangered.

No indeed! This was not the reason why James Ensor etched, even if he saw etching as a means of multiplying his drawings and making a profit from them. Had he not capitulated to his particular style of humor, he would certainly have said instead that "I have etched, I have made drypoints and lithographs, because they please me as an artist, because along with my dedication to and love of color and painting, I carry within me a worship for the line, or rather worship for and love of the different sorts of lines which enchant, move, and allure, just as the notes, or phrases, of different musical instruments enchant, move, and allure. I carry within me the worship and love of drawn lines, with their touch—sometimes thick and indistinct, sometimes fine and leaden gray, sometimes soft, stippled, and stressed; within me I carry the dedication to and love of engraved line, capriciously incised in metal or hollowed directly into the copper with a needle, which makes them sharper—the dedication to and love of engraved lines, which spread ink on paper with reflections and intensities which have no parallel. I search for the linear, because it allows me to portray in an eloquent language and in forms that are acutely alive what stirs me, what I see, and what I want."

If James Ensor did not wish to make this statement himself, we do it for him to pay him homage. Without this dedication, this love of color as well as line, he would never have become—nor have remained—one of our greatest painters, one of our greatest draftsmen, one our greatest etchers.

LOUIS LEBEER

CONTENTS

The Prints of JAMES ENSOR

From the Collection of H. Shickman

All measurements in millimeters, height by width

Abbreviations:

S.I.P. ...... Signed in Plate

D. .... Delteil, Loys. *Le Peintre graveur illustré.* Vol. XIX. Paris: The Author, 1925 [Reprint edition. New York: Da Capo Press, 1969].

L. .... Lebeer, Louis. *Notes pour servir de complément au catalogue de l'oeuvre gravé de James Ensor.* Brussels: Van der Perre, 1939.

C. .... Croquez, Albert, *L'oeuvre gravé de James Ensor.* Geneva and Brussels: Editions Pierre Cailler, 1947.

1

The Mocking of Christ (Christ Shown to the People)
   (1886)
Le Christ insulté (Jesus montré au peuple)
237 x 160
Etching and drypoint
S.I.P. lower left "Ensor 1886"
Pencil signed lower right "James Ensor 1886"
D.1, 2nd state; C.1, 2nd state

2

Orchard (in Oudenbourg) (1886)

Le Verger (à Oudenbourg)

Etching

161 x 240

S.I.P. lower right "Ensor 1886"

Titled in pencil lower left "Le Verger"; pencil signed lower
   right "James Ensor 1886"

D.2; C.2, 2nd state

3

Portrait of the Swedish Botanist Frise (The
    Ancestor) (1886)
Portrait de Frise, botaniste suedois (L'ancêtre)
Etching
246 x 184
S.I.P. lower right "Ensor 1886"
Pencil signed lower right "James Ensor 1886"
D.3; C.3, 2nd state

4

Self-Portrait (1886)
L'artiste par lui-meme
Etching
100 x 70
S.I.P. lower left "Ensor"
Pencil signed lower right "James Ensor 1886"
D.4, 2nd state; C.4, 2nd state

5

Christ Calming the Storm (1886)
Le Christ apaisant la tempête
Etching and drypoint
160 x 238
S.I.P. lower left "Ensor"; lower right "J. Ensor"
Pencil signed lower right "James Ensor 1886"
D.5, 3rd state; C.5, 3rd state

6

Iston, Pouffamatus, Cracozie, and Transmouff, Famous
  Persian Physicians Examine the Excrements of King
  Darius After the Battle of Arbella (1886)
*Iston, Pouffamatus, Cracozie et Transmouff, célèbres
  médecins persans examinant les selles du roi Darius après
  la bataille d'Arbelles*

Etching
243 x 185
S.I.P. lower left "Ensor 86"
Pencil signed lower right "James Ensor 1886"
D.6 (undescribed state 2b); L. 2nd state; C.6, 3d state

7

The Cathedral (1886)

La cathédrale

Etching

246 x 190

S.I.P. upper right "Ensor 1886"

Pencil signed lower right "James Ensor 1886"

D.7, 2nd state; C.7, 2nd state

7b

The Cathedral (2nd plate) (1886)
La cathédrale (2e planche)
Etching
250 x 190
S.I.P. upper right "Ensor 1886"
Pencil signed lower right "James Ensor"
D.105; C.7b

8

The Magdalene (1887)

La Madeleine

Drypoint

280 x 188

S.I.P. lower left "Ensor 87"

Pencil signed lower right "James Ensor 1887"

D.9; L. 2nd state; C.9, 2nd state

9

Infernal Procession (Devils on the Way to a
    Sabbath) (1887)
Cortège infernal (Diables se rendant au Sabbat)
Etching
214 x 266
S.I.P. upper right "Ensor"; lower left hand margin "Ensor 8"
Pencil signed lower right "James Ensor 1887"
D.10; C.10

10

**Portrait of Ernest Rousseau, Rector of the
    University in Brussels** (1887)
*Portrait d'Ernest Rousseau, recteur de l'Université Libre
    de Bruxelles*
Drypoint
240 x 181
S.I.P. lower right "Ensor 87"
Pencil signed lower right "James Ensor 1887"
D.11, 2nd state; C.11, 2nd state

11

A Man of the People (1887)
Un homme du peuple
Etching
149 x 108
Pencil signed lower right "James Ensor 1887"
D.12; C.12

12

Large View of Mariakerke (1887)

Grande vue de Mariakerke

Etching

215 x 270

Pencil signed lower right "James Ensor 1887"

D.13; L. 2nd state; C.13, 2nd state

13

Docks in Ostende (1887)
L'estacade à Ostende
Drypoint
89 x 128
S.I.P. lower right "J. Ensor"
Pencil signed lower right "James Ensor"
D.14; C.14, 1st state

14

Sleeping Woman (The Artist's Mother) (1887)
La dormeuse (Mère de l'artiste)

Drypoint

90 x 123

Titled in pencil lower left "La dormeuse"; pencil signed
  lower right "James Ensor"

D.15, 2nd state; C.15, 2nd state

15

Small View of Mariakerke (1887)
Petite vue de Mariakerke
Etching and drypoint
89 x 129
S.I.P. lower right "Ensor"
Pencil signed lower right "James Ensor 1887"
D.16, 2nd state; C.16, 2nd state

16

Rue du Bon-Secours in Brussels (1887)
Rue du Bon-Secours à Bruxelles

Drypoint
128 x 89
Pencil signed lower right "James Ensor"
D.17; C.17

17

Bust (after a sculpture by Jef Lambeaux which stood on
    Rousseau's fireplace) (1887)
*Buste (d'après une sculpture de Jef Lambeaux qui se trouvait
    sur la cheminée du salon des Rousseau)*

Drypoint
130 x 88
Pencil signed lower right "James Ensor 1887"
D.18; C.18

18

Battle of the Beggars Désir and Rissolé (1888)
Combat des pouilleux Désir et Rissolé

Drypoint
236 x 290
S.I.P. lower left "Ensor 88"; lower center "Ensor 1888"
Pencil signed lower right "James Ensor 1888"
D.19, 2nd state; C.19, 2nd state

19

Houses on the Boulevard Anspach in Brussels (1888)
Maisons du boulevard Anspach à Bruxelles
Drypoint
139 x 92
Pencil signed lower right "James Ensor 1888"
D.20; L. 3d state; C.20, 3d state

20

Edge of the Forest in Ostende (1888)
La lisière du petit bois, Ostende
Etching
80 x 118
S.I.P. lower left "ENSOR"
Pencil signed lower right "James Ensor"
D.27, 3d state; C.21, 3d state

21

Street Lantern (1888)

Le Réverbère

Etching

97 x 69

S.I.P. upper right "ENSOR"

Pencil signed lower right "James Ensor"

D.21, 2nd state; C.22, 2nd state

22

The Haunted Closet (1888)
Le meuble hanté
Etching
140 x 90
S.I.P. lower left "Ensor"
Pencil signed lower right "James Ensor 1888"
D.22, 3d state; C.23, 3rd state

23

Devils Beating Angels and Archangels (Fight of the
 Demons) (1888)
Diables rossant anges et archanges (Le combat des demons)
Etching
260 x 314
S.I.P. lower right "Ensor 88"
Titled in pencil lower left "Diables rossant anges et
 archanges. vision devançant le futurisme"; pencil signed
 lower right "James Ensor 1888"
D.23; C.24

24

The Acacia (1888)
L'acacia
Drypoint
141 x 92
S.I.P. upper left "Ensor 88"
Pencil signed lower right "James Ensor"
D.24, 2nd state; C.25, 2nd state

25

The Chimera (after a small grotesque in white enamel;
   lower left the head of Rousseau's son) (1888)
La chimère (d'après un petit monstre en émail blanc;
   la tête à gauche en bas est celle du fils Rousseau)
Etching
100 x 68
Pencil signed lower right "James Ensor 1888"
D.25; C.26

26

The Crypt (of the St. Bavon Church in Ghent) (1888)
La crypte (de l'église Saint-Bavon à Gand)

Drypoint
137 x 98
S.I.P. lower left "Ensor"
Pencil signed lower right "James Ensor 1888"
D.26; C.27

27

The City Hall in Audenarde (1888)
L'hôtel de ville d'Audenarde
Etching
159 x 118
S.I.P. lower right "J. ENSOR 1888 AUDENAERDE"
Pencil signed lower right "James Ensor"
D.28, 2nd state; C.28, 2nd state

28

Skulls and Masks (A Nightmare) (1888)
Cranes et masques (Un cauchemar)
Etching
99 x 138
S.I.P. lower right "Ensor"
Pencil signed lower right "James Ensor 1888"
D.29; C.29 (undescribed state)

29

The Channel of Nieuport (1888)

Le chenal de Nieuport

Etching

89 x 137

S.I.P. lower right "Ensor"

Pencil signed lower right "James Ensor"

D.30; C.30

30

Candelabra and Vase (1888)

Candélabre et vase

Etching and drypoint

120 x 80

S.I.P. lower right "Ensor"

Pencil signed lower right "James Ensor 1888"

D.31; C.31

31

Capture of a Strange Town (1888)
Prise d'une ville étrange
Etching
176 x 237
S.I.P. on the lower right margin "Ensor"; at the lower right
    margin (on the back of a figure) "Ensor"
Pencil signed lower right "James Ensor 1888"
D.33, 3d state; C.33, 2nd state

32

My Portrait in the Year 1960 (1888)
Mon portrait en 1960 (Simple anticipation)
Etching
69 x 120
S.I.P. lower right "Ensor"
Pencil signed lower right "James Ensor 1888"
D.34; C.34

33

My Father on His Death-Bed (1888)
Mon père mort
Etching and drypoint
99 x 139
S.I.P. lower left "Ensor"
Pencil signed lower right "James Ensor 1888"
D.35, 2nd state; C.35, 2nd state

34

The Terrible Archer (1888)

L'archer terrible

Etching

175 x 236

S.I.P. lower right "Ensor"

Titled in pencil lower left "L'archer terrible"; pencil signed
    lower right "James Ensor 1888"

D.36, 2nd state; C.36, 2nd state

35

The Cataclysms (1888)

Les cataclysmes

Etching

179 x 238

S.I.P. lower right "Ensor"

Pencil signed lower right "James Ensor 1888"

D.37; C.37

36

The Murder (Recollection of the famous crime of
    Rodez in which the agent Fualdès was killed) (1888)
L'assasinat (Reminiscence du crime célèbre de Rodez,
    où l'agent d'affaires Fualdès a trouvé la mort)

Etching
180 x 240
S.I.P. lower right "J. Ensor"
Pencil signed lower right "James Ensor 1888"
D.38; C.38

37

The Port of Ostende (1888)
Vue du port d'Ostende
Etching
80 x 119
S.I.P. lower right "Ensor"
Pencil signed lower right "James Ensor 1888"
D.39; C.39, 1st state

38

Ostende as Seen From the East (1888)
Vue d'Ostende, à l'est

Etching
90 x 139
S.I.P. lower right "J. Ensor"
Pencil signed lower right "James Ensor 1888"
D.40, 2nd state; C.40, 2nd state

39

Group of Trees (1888)
Bouquet d'arbres
Etching
100 x 139
S.I.P. lower right "Ensor"
Pencil signed lower right "James Ensor"
D. 41, 2nd state; C.41, 2nd state

40

Flemish Farm (1888)

Ferme flamande

Etching

80 x 118

S.I.P. lower left "Ensor"

Pencil signed lower right "James Ensor"

D.42; C.42

41

Bizarre Musicians (1888)
Musiciens fantastiques
Etching
175 x 236
S.I.P. lower left "Ensor"
Pencil signed lower right "James Ensor 1888"
D.43; C.43, 1st state

42

The Fishing Docks in Ostende (1888)
Les chaloupes (Coin du bassin des pêcheurs à Ostende)
Etching
177 x 235
S.I.P. lower left "Ensor"
Pencil signed lower right "James Ensor"
D.44; C.44, 1st state

43

Large Basin of Ostende Harbor (1888)

Le grand bassin d'Ostende

Etching

178 x 257

S.I.P. lower right "Ensor 88"

D.45; L. 3rd state; C.45, 3rd state

44

Strange Insects (Madame Rousseau and Ensor) (1888)
Insects singuliers (Madame Rousseau et Ensor)
Drypoint
119 x 159
S.I.P. upper left "Ensor 1888"; lower right "Ensor 88"
Pencil signed lower right "James Ensor 1888"
D.46, 5th state; C.46, 4th state

45

A Gust of Wind at the Edge of the Forest (on the property
   of Rousseau at Watermael near Brussels) (1888)
Coup de vent à la lisière (dans la propriété des Rousseau
   à Watermael, près de Bruxelles)

Etching
177 x 248
S.I.P. lower left "Ensor 88"
Pencil signed lower right "James Ensor"
D.47, 2nd state; C.47, 2nd state

46

Path in Groenendael (1888)
Sentier à Groenendael
Etching
137 x 100
S.I.P. lower center "Ensor 1888"
Pencil signed lower right "James Ensor"
D.48, 2nd state; C.48, 2nd state

47

Boats at Low Tide (1888)

Les barques echouées

Etching

179 x 238

S.I.P. lower right "Ensor 1888"

Pencil signed lower right "James Ensor"

D.49, 2nd state; L. 3rd state; C.49, 2nd state

48

Thatched Cottages (in Slykens near Ostende) (1888)
Chaumières (à Slykens, près d'Ostende)
Etching
120 x 79
S.I.P. upper right "Ensor 1888"
Pencil signed lower right "James Ensor 1888"
D.50; C.50

49

Tormenting the Elephant (1888)

La blague de l'éléphant

Etching

180 x 238

S.I.P. lower right "Ensor"

Pencil signed lower right "James Ensor 1888"

D.51; C.51

50

Wizards in the Whirlwind (The Winds) (1888)
Sorciers dans la bourrasque (Les vents)
Etching
173 x 236
S.I.P. lower right "Ensor"
Pencil signed lower right "James Ensor 1888"
D.52, 2nd state; C.52, 2nd state

51

Small Bizarre Figures (My friends transformed into
    animals. The Rousseau family and Ensor) (1888)
Petites figures bizarres (Mes amis animalisés. Les Rousseau
    et Ensor)
Etching
139 x 99
S.I.P. lower right "Ensor"
Pencil signed lower right "James Ensor 1888"
D.53, 2nd state; C.53, 2nd state

52

Small Houses in Mariakerke (1888)

Maisonnettes à Mariakerke

Etching

78 x 121

S.I.P. lower right "Ensor"

Pencil signed lower right "James Ensor"

D.54, 2nd state; C.54, 2nd state

53

The Policemen (Memories of a Strike in Ostende) (1888)
Les Gendarmes (Souvenir d'une grève à Ostende)
Etching and drypoint
179 x 238
S.I.P. lower left "Ensor"
Pencil signed lower right "James Ensor 1888"
D.55, 4th state; C.55, 3d state

54

Flayed Man (1888)

L'écorché

Etching

138 x 100

S.I.P. upper right "Ensor"

Pencil signed lower right "James Ensor 1888"

D.57; C.57, 1st state

55

Adoration of the Shepherds (1888)

L'adoration des bergers

Etching and drypoint

160 x 118

S.I.P. lower left "ENSOR 1888"

Pencil signed lower right "James Ensor 1888"

D.58, 2nd state; C.58, 2nd state

56

Lust (1888)

La luxure

Etching

98 x 137

S.I.P. lower left "ENSOR"; lower right "Ensor"

Titled in pencil lower left "Luxure"; pencil signed lower
    right "James Ensor 1888"

D.59, 2nd state; C.59, 2nd state

56b Not illustrated

Hand-colored impression of number 56 (watercolor)

Pencil signed lower right "James Ensor"

57

Temptation of Christ (1888)

La tentation du Christ

Etching

80 x 119

S.I.P. upper right "Ensor"

Pencil signed lower right "James Ensor"

D.60; C.60

58

The Garden of Love (1888)
Le jardin d'amour
Etching
118 x 80
S.I.P. lower center "Ensor"
Pencil signed lower right "James Ensor 1888"
D.61, 2nd state; C.61, 2nd state

59

Caesar's Coin (1888)

Le denier de César

Etching

138 x 179

S.I.P. upper right "Ensor 88"

Titled in pencil lower margin "Le denier de César. Rendez
    à César ce que revient à César et à Dieu ce que revient
    à Dieu"; pencil signed lower right "James Ensor 1888"

D.62; C.62

60

Under the Trees in Groenendael near Brussels (1888)
Sous-bois à Groenendael, près de Bruxelles

Drypoint
119 x 80
S.I.P. upper right "ENSOR"
Pencil signed lower right "James Ensor 1888"
D.63, 3d state; C.63, 3d state

61

Steamboats (in the Ostende Harbor) (1888)
Bateaux à vapeur (dans un des bassins d'Ostende)
Etching
76 x 118
S.I.P. at the lower right hand margin "ENSOR"
Pencil signed lower right "James Ensor 1889"
D.64, 3d state; C.64, 2nd state

62

The Ice Skaters (on the property of the Rousseau family
in Watermael near Brussels) (1889)
*Les patineurs (dans la propriété des Rousseau à Watermael
près de Bruxelles)*

Etching and drypoint
178 x 239
S.I.P. lower right "Ensor 1889"
Pencil signed lower right "James Ensor 1889"
D.65, 2nd state; C.65, 2nd state

63

Boulevard van Iseghem in Ostende (View from Ensor's
    Old Studio) (1889)
Le boulevard van Iseghem à Ostende
(Vue prise de l'ancien atelier d'Ensor)
Etching
140 x 100
S.I.P. lower right "Ensor 1889"
Pencil signed lower right "James Ensor"
D.66; C.66

64

Self-portrait as a Skeleton (1889)

Mon portrait squelettisé

Etching

120 x 79

S.I.P. lower left "ENSOR"

Pencil signed lower right "James Ensor 1889"

D.67, 3d state; C.67, 3d state

65

Farm in Leffinghe (*c.* One Mile from Ostende) (1889)
Ferme à Leffinghe (à une lieue d'Ostende)
Etching
80 x 119
S.I.P. lower right "ENSOR"
Pencil signed lower right "James Ensor"
D.68, 2nd state; C.68, 2nd state

66

The Bridge in the Woods, Ostende (1889)
Le pont du bois à Ostende
Etching
98 x 139
S.I.P. lower left "ENSOR" (in reverse)
Pencil signed lower right "James Ensor"
D.69; C.69, 2nd state

67

The Thunderstorm (1889)
L'orage
Etching
80 x 120
S.I.P. lower right "Ensor"
Pencil signed lower right "James Ensor 1889"
D.70, 2nd state; C.70, 2nd state

68

Country Fair Near a Windmill (in Oudenburg) (1889)

Le kermesse au moulin (à Oudenburg)

Etching

138 x 178

S.I.P. upper left "Ensor"

Pencil signed lower right "James Ensor"

D.72; C.72

69

The Phantom (Vision of a Sage Taken for a Fool) (1889)
Le fantôme (Vision d'un sage, qu'on a pris pour un fou)
Etching
80 x 120
S.I.P. lower right "ENSOR"
Pencil signed lower right "James Ensor 1889"
D.73, 1st state; C.73, 2nd state

70

Swamp with Poplars (Part of the Woods in Ostende)
   (1889)
La mare aux peupliers (Coin du boise d'Ostende)
Etching
160 x 239
S.I.P. upper right "Ensor 1889"
Pencil signed lower right "James Ensor"
D.74; C.74

71

The Fantastic Ball (1889)
Le bal fantastique
Etching
79 x 120
S.I.P. lower center "Ensor"
Pencil signed lower right "James Ensor 1889
D.75, 1st state; C.75, 1st state

71b Not illustrated
Different state of number 71
Pencil signed lower right "James Ensor 1889"
W.75, 2nd state; C.75, 2nd state

72

Rustic Bridge (1889)

Le pont rustique

Etching and drypoint

78 x 119

S.I.P. upper left "ENSOR"

Pencil signed lower right "James Ensor 1889"

D.76, 2nd state; C.76, 2nd state

73

The Exterminating Angel (1889)

L'ange exterminateur

Etching

118 x 157

S.I.P. upper right "Ensor"

Pencil signed lower right "James Ensor 1889"

D.77; C.77

74

The Triumphal March of the Romans (1889)
Le triomphe romain
Etching and drypoint
177 x 239
S.I.P. lower left "Ensor"
Pencil signed lower right "James Ensor 1889"
D.78, 2nd state; C.78, 2nd state

75

Forced-Feeding (2nd Plate) (1889)
Alimentation doctrinaire (2e planche)·

Etching

178 x 248

Titled in plate upper right "BELGIQUE EN 1889
    ALIMENTATION DOCTRINAIRE"; S.I.P. lower right
    "J. Ensor 1889"

Pencil signed and titled lower right "James Ensor 1889
    Alimentation doctrinaire"

D.96; C.80

76

Hector Denis (Socialist Deputy) (1890)
Hector Denis (député socialiste)
Etching
122 x 78
Titled in plate lower left "A. Hector Denis"; S.I.P. lower
    right "James Ensor 1890"
Pencil signed lower right "James Ensor 1890"
D.80; C.82, 2nd state

77

Music in the Rue de Flandre in Ostende (1890)
Musique, rue de Flandre à Ostende
Etching
118 x 78
S.I.P. upper right "Ensor 1890"
Pencil signed lower right "James Ensor"
D.81; L. 2nd state; C.83, 2nd state

78

Windmill in Slykens (Near Ostende) (1891)
Le moulin de Slykens (près d'Ostende)
Etching
70 x 100
S.I.P. upper left "Ensor"
Pencil signed lower right "James Ensor"
D.82; C.84

79

Feeding of the Five Thousand (1891)

La multiplication des poissons

Etching

178 x 237

S.I.P. lower left "Ensor 1891"

Pencil singed lower right "James Ensor 1891"

D.83; C.85

80

Autodafé
(with the image of Philippe II, King of Spain, after a coin)
(Philippe II in Hell) (1893)
Autodafé (avec l'effigie de Philippe II, roi d'Espagne, d'aprés
une pièce do monnaie) (Phillipe II aux enfers)

Etching
87 x 121
S.I.P. lower right "Ensor 1893"
Pencil signed lower right "James Ensor"
D.85; C.87

81

The Good Judges (1894)
Les bons juges
Etching and drypoint
179 x 239
S.I.P. lower left "ENSOR"
Pencil signed lower right "James Ensor 1894"
D.86, 2nd state; L. 2nd state; C.88, 2nd state

82

Small Boats (1894)
Les petites barques
Etching and drypoint
90 x 142
S.I.P. lower right "Ensor 94"
Pencil signed lower right "James Ensor 1894"
D.87; C.89

83

Christ in Hell (The Devils Dzitts and Hihanox Lead
   Christ into Hell) (1895)
*Le Christ aux enfers (Les diables Dzitts et Hihanox
   conduisant le Christ aux enfers)*
Etching and drypoint
139 x 178
S.I.P. lower left "Ensor 95"
Pencil signed lower right "James Ensor 1895"
D.88; C.90

Beggar Warming Himself (1895)

Pouilleux se chauffant

Etching

159 x 118

Titled in plate upper center "Pouilleux indispose se
    chauffant"; S.I.P. lower right "J. Ensor 1895"

Pencil signed lower right "James Ensor"

D.89; C.91

85

The Gamblers (1895)
Les joueurs
Etching
118 x 159
S.I.P. lower left "Ensor"
Pencil signed lower right "James Ensor 1895"
D.92; C.92

86

Demons Taunting Me (1895)

Démons me turlupinant

Etching

118 x 158

S.I.P. upper center "J. Ensor 1895"

Pencil signed lower right "James Ensor 1895"

D.91; C.93

87

Christ Tormented by Demons (The Agony of Christ)
(1895)
Le Christ tourmenté par les démons (Le Christ agonisant)
Etching and drypoint
179 x 242
S.I.P. lower left "JAMES ENSOR 1895"
Pencil signed lower right "James Ensor 1895"
D.93; C.94

88

Fridolin and Gragapança D'Yperdam (Eug. Demolder
   and J. Ensor) (1895)
*Fridolin et Gragapança D'Yperdam (Eug. Demolder et
   J. Ensor)*
Etching and drypoint
101 x 140
Titled in plate upper center "Fridolin et Gragapança
   d'Yperdamme"; S.I.P. lower right "J. Ensor 1895"
Pencil signed lower right "JAMES ENSOR, 1895"
D.94; C.95

89

Battle of the Golden Spurs (1895)

Bataille des Eperons d'Or

Etching

241 x 280

S.I.P. lower center "J. Ensor"

Titled in pencil lower left "La Bataille des Eperons d'Or";
    pencil signed lower right "James Ensor 1895"

D. 95; C.96

90

The Wicked Physicians (1895)

Les mauvais médecins

Etching and drypoint

178 x 252

Titled in plate upper center "Les mauvais medecins";
    S.I.P. lower left "J. Ensor 95"

Pencil signed lower right "J. Ensor 1895"

D.97; C.97

91

Skeletons Warming Themselves (1895)

Squelettes voulant se chauffer

Etching

139 x 102

Titled in plate upper margin "squelettes voulant se chauffer";
   S.I.P. lower right "J. Ensor 95"

Pencil signed lower right "James Ensor 1895"

D.98; C.98, 1st state

92

Angry Masks (1895)

Masques scandalisés

Etching

119 x 83

Titled in plate on upper margin "Masques Scandalisés";
   S.I.P. lower left "J. Ensor 95"

Pencil signed lower right "James Ensor 1895"

D.99; C.99

93

King Pest (1895)

Le roi Peste

Etching

100 x 120

S.I.P. lower left "J. Ensor 95"

Pencil signed lower right "James Ensor"

D.100; C.100

94

Christ and the Beggars (1895)

Le Christ aux mendiants

Etching

93 x 142

S.I.P. lower right "Ensor 95"

Pencil signed lower right "James Ensor"

D.102, 2nd state; C.101

95

The Doctors' Visit (The Old . . . Pigs) (1895)
La visite des medecins (Les vieux . . . polissons)
Etching and drypoint
102 x 142
S.I.P. lower right "J. Ensor 95"
Pencil signed lower right "James Ensor 1895"
D.101; C.102

96

Christ Descending into Hell (2nd version) (1895)
Le Christ descendant aux enfers (2me version)
Etching
90 x 143
S.I.P. upper right "J. Ensor 95"
Pencil signed lower right "James Ensor 1895"
D.103; L. 2nd state; C.103, 2nd state

97

Death Pursuing Humanity (1896)

La mort poursuivant le troupeau des humains

Etching

241 x 182

S.I.P. lower left "J. Ensor"

Titled in pencil lower left "La mort poursuivant le troupeau
   des humains"; pencil signed lower right "James Ensor
   1896"

D.104; C.104, 1st state

98

The Scavenger (1896)

Le vidangeur

Etching

121 x 84

S.I.P. lower right "J. Ensor"

Pencil signed lower right "James Ensor 1896"

D.106; C.105

99

The Vagabonds (1896)

Les sacripants

Etching

120 x 83

S.I.P. lower left "J. Ensor"

Pencil signed lower right "James Ensor 1896"

D.108; C.106

100

The Fight (1896)
Le combat
Etching
120 x 85
S.I.P. lower left "J. Ensor"
Pencil signed lower right "James Ensor 1896"
D.107; C.107

101

Menu for Ernest Rousseau (1896)
Menu pour Ernest Rousseau
Etching and drypoint
183 x 135
S.I.P. lower left "J. Ensor"
Pencil signed lower right "James Ensor 1896"
D.109; C.108

102

Menu for Charles Vos (1896)
Menu pour Charles Vos
Etching
157 x 109
S.I.P. lower right "Ensor"
Pencil signed lower right "James Ensor 1896"
D.110; C.109

103

Napoleon's Farewell (1897)

Les adieux de Napoleon

Etching

122 x 189

S.I.P. lower left "Ensor 97"

Pencil signed lower right "James Ensor 1897"

D.111, 2nd state; C.110

104

Hop Frog's Revenge

La vengeance de Hop-Frog

Etching

359 x 251

S.I.P. lower center (on the back of a figure) "ENSOR 98"

Pencil signed lower right "James Ensor"

D.112, 2nd state; C.111, 2nd state

105

Christ in a Boat (1898)
Le Christ dans la barque
Etching
84 x 119
S.I.P. lower right "Ensor"
Pencil signed lower right "James Ensor"
D.113; C.113

106

The Entry of Christ into Brussels (1898)

L'entrée du Christ à Bruxelles

Etching

249 x 358

S.I.P. lower right "J. Ensor"

Pencil signed lower right "James Ensor 1898"

D.114, 2nd state; C.114 2nd state

107

Beach in Ostende (1899)

Les bains à Ostende

Etching and drypoint
224 x 279
S.I.P. lower right "Ensor"
Pencil signed lower right "James Ensor 1899"
D.115; C.115, 2nd state

108

Small View of Mariakerke (2nd plate) (1900)
Petite vue de Mariakerke (2e planche)

Etching
75 x 113
S.I.P. lower right "Ensor"
Pencil signed lower right "James Ensor 1900"
D.117; C.116

109

Queen Parysatis (Part of the Temptation of St. Anthony)
  (1900)
La reine Parysatis (Fragment de la Tentation de St. Antoine)
Etching
170 x 120
S.I.P. lower center "ENSOR"
Pencil signed lower right "James Ensor 1900"
D.116 (undescribed state); C.117, 1st state

109b Not illustrated
Different state of number 109
Pencil signed lower right "James Ensor 1900"
D.116; C.117, 2nd state

110

Fisherman from Ostende (1900)

Pêcheur d'Ostende

Etching

140 x 100

Titled in plate upper left "Ostende"; S.I.P. lower center
    "Ensor"

Pencil signed lower right "James Ensor 1900"

D.118; L. 2nd state; C.118 (undescribed state 1b)

111

Laziness (1902)

La paresse

Etching

100 x 140

Titled in plate lower left "Paresse"; S.I.P. lower right
  "Ensor"

Pencil signed lower right "James Ensor 1902"

D.119, 2nd state; C.119, 2nd state

111b Not illustrated

Hand-colored impression of number 111 (water color and
  gouache)

Pencil signed lower right "James Ensor"

112

The Roofs of Ostende (1903)
Les toits d'Ostende
Etching
100 x 149
S.I.P. lower right "Ensor"
Pencil signed lower right "James Ensor 1903"
D.120 (undescribed state 2b); C.120 (undescribed state 2b)

113

Temper (1904)

La colère

Etching

98 x 150

S.I.P. lower right "Ensor"

Titled in pencil lower left "Colere"; pencil signed lower
 right "James Ensor 1904"

D.121, 2nd state; C.121, 2nd state

113b Not illustrated

Hand-colored impression of number 113 (watercolor and
 gouache)

Pencil signed lower right "James Ensor"

114

Pride (1904)

L'orgueil

Etching

98 x 150

S.I.P. lower right "Ensor"

Titled in pencil lower left "orgueil"; pencil signed lower
right "James Ensor 1904"

D.122, 4th state; C.122, 3d state

114b Not illustrated

Hand-colored impression of number 114 (watercolor and
gouache)

Pencil signed lower right "James Ensor"

115

Avarice (1904)

L'avarice

Etching

98 x 150

S.I.P. lower left "Ensor"

Titled in pencil lower right "avarice"; pencil signed lower
   right "James Ensor 1904"

D.123, 2nd state; C.123, 2nd state

115b Not illustrated

Hand-colored impression of number 115 (watercolor and
   gouache)

Pencil signed lower right "James Ensor"

116

Gluttony (1904)

La gourmandise

Etching

98 x 150

S.I.P. lower right "Ensor"

Titled in pencil lower left "Gourmandise"; pencil signed
   lower right "James Ensor 1904"

D.124; C.124

116b Not illustrated

Hand-colored impression of number 116 (watercolor and
   gouache)

Pencil signed lower right "James Ensor"

117

Envy (1904)
L'envie
Etching
98 x 150
S.I.P. upper right "Ensor"
Titled in pencil lower left "Envie"; pencil signed lower
    right "James Ensor 1904"
D.125, 3d state; C.125, 3d state

117b Not illustrated
Hand-colored impression of number 117 (watercolor and
  gouache)
Pencil signed lower right "James Ensor"

118 Pride greed envy lust gluttony tempes sloth

Death Dominating the Deadly Sins (1904)

Les péchés capitaux dominés par la mort

Etching

90 x 140

S.I.P. lower right "Ensor"

Titled in pencil lower left "Péchés capitaux dominés par la
   mort"; pencil signed lower right "James Ensor 1904"

D.126; C.126

118b Not illustrated

Hand-colored impression of number 118 (watercolor and
   gouache)

Pencil signed lower right "James Ensor 1903"

119

Plague Below, Plague Above, Plague Everywhere (1904)

Peste dessous, peste dessus, peste partout

Etching

197 x 298

Titled in plate at top "Peste Dessous Peste Dessus Peste
    Partout"; S.I.P. lower right "Ensor"

Pencil signed lower right "James Ensor 1904"

D.127; C.127

120

Intriguing Masks (1904)

Masques intrigués

Etching

80 x 119

S.I.P. lower left "Ensor"

Pencil signed lower right "James Ensor 1904"

D.128; C.128

121

Beach at La Panne (1904)

Plage de la Panne

Etching

101 x 150

S.I.P. lower right "Ensor"

Titled in pencil lower left "La Plage de la Panne"; pencil
   signed lower right "James Ensor 1904"

D.129; C.129

SUPPLEMENT

Ensor Prints Not Available in the Shickman Collection

A

The Flagellation (1886)
La Flagellation
Etching
96 x 64
S.I.P. upper left "Ensor 86"
D.8; C.8

B

The Hunter (1888)
Le Chasseur
Etching
119 x 159
S.I.P. lower left "J.E."
D.32; C.32

C

Starry Night at the Cemetery (1888)
Les étoiles au cimetière
Etching
139 x 180
D.56; C.56

D

Windmill at Mariakerke (1889)
Le moulin de Mariakerke
Etching
129 x 179
D.71; C.71

E. Forced Feeding (1st plate) (1889)
Alimentation doctrinaire (1re planche)
Etching
180 x 240
D.79; C.79
Not illustrated. No impressions have been
located, although the zinc plate exists.

F

Nineteenth Century Belgium (1889)
La Belgique au XIXe siècle
Etching
163 x 241
S.I.P. lower left "Ensor"
C.81

G

Hop Frog's Revenge (1898)
Hop Frog's Revenge
Lithograph
377 x 277
D.130; C.112

H

Lady Godiva(1933)
Lady Godiva
Drypoint
125 x 88
S.I.P. lower right "Ensor 33"
C.130

I

The Old House (1933)
La vieille maison
Drypoint
180 x 130
C.131

J

Procession at Ghistelles (1934)
La procession de Ghistelles
Drypoint
C.132

K

The Devil at the Mill (1934)
Le diable au moulin
Soft-ground etching
148 x 192
S.I.P. lower right "Ensor 34"
C.133

INDEX OF PRINTS

James Sidney Ensor

1860–1949

1860	Born, Ostend, Belgium, April 13.
1873	Enters Collège Notre-Dame, Ostend; poor student, begins to draw. Drawing lessons with watercolorists Dubar and Vankuyck.
1876	First paintings: small outdoor works on cardboard (dunes, sea, countryside).
1877	Enters Brussels Academy; meets Crespin, Charlet, Duyck. Paints academic study, *The Model*.
1879	*Girl with the Turned-up Nose*: beginning of so-called "somber period." First mask painting: *Mask Gazing at a Negro Mountebank*. Meets Ernest Rousseau.
1880	Leaves Brussels Academy; settles at Ostend. Draws *Mystic Death of a Theologian*; series of charcoal drawings of ordinary local types. Paints *The Lamp Boy, Lady with a Fan, The Colorist*.
1881	Exhibits with La Chrysalide group, Brussels. *Portrait of the Artist's Father, Russian Music, Afternoon at Ostend, The Bourgeois Salon, Somber Lady*.
1882	*Woman Eating Oysters* rejected by Antwerp Salon. Exhibits at Cercle Artistique, Brussels.
1883	Exhibits with avant-garde group, L'Essor; joins avant-garde group, Les XX.
1884	Brussels Salon rejects all his work. *White Cloud, Ostend Rooftops*.
1885	*Skeletons Looking at Chinoiseries*; large drawing, *Hail Jesus, King of the Jews*. Hostility of critics mounts.
1886	Completes first etchings: *Christ Mocked, Christ Calming the Waters, The Cathedral*.
1887	Death of his father: series of deathbed drawings. "Light period" now begins.
1888–1890	Les XX now reject his works. *The Entrance of Christ into Brussels, Intrigue*.
1891	*Skeletons Fighting for the Body of the Hanged Man, The Tragic Musicians, Melancholy Fishwives, The Judges*, and others.
1892	Short visit to London.
1896	Eugène Demolder organizes first Ensor exhibition, Brussels.
1898	*La Plume* organizes small exhibition in Paris.
1900	Production of work slows down.

1901	*Kermesse with Blood Sausages* completed; member, Libre Académie de Belgique.
1903	Named Knight of Order of Leopold.
1904	Series of etchings, including, *Peste dessus, peste dessous, peste partout*, and *Seven Deadly Sins*.
1906	François Franck, Antwerp art patron, becomes his champion.
1911	Writes and designs ballet, *La Gamme d'amour*; Emil Nolde visits him.
1912	Series of *Life of Christ* drawings.
1913	*War of the Snails* drawing.
1915	Death of his mother; draws and paints her. Large decorative panel: *The Mask Is Off*.
1920	Retrospective show at Giroux Gallery, Brussels. *Christ among the Doctors*.
1921	Retrospective show, Salon de l'Art contemporain, Antwerp.
1925	*Rape of Andromeda*.
1926	First important Paris exhibition, at Galerie Barbazanges.
1929	Subject of inaugural exhibition of Palais des Beaux-Arts, Brussels.
1932	Exhibition at Jeu de Paume Museum, Paris.
1933	Named commander of Légion d'Honneur.
1938	Principal figure in founding of Les Compagnons de l'Art.
1939	Paris exhibition organized by *La Gazette des Beaux-Arts*.
1946	Retrospective show at National Gallery, London.
1948	Les Amis de James Ensor, club devoted to his art, is formed.
1949	Dies, Ostend, November 19.